My Vicissitudes

A Journey Through

Mental Illness * Becoming Estranged * Contentment

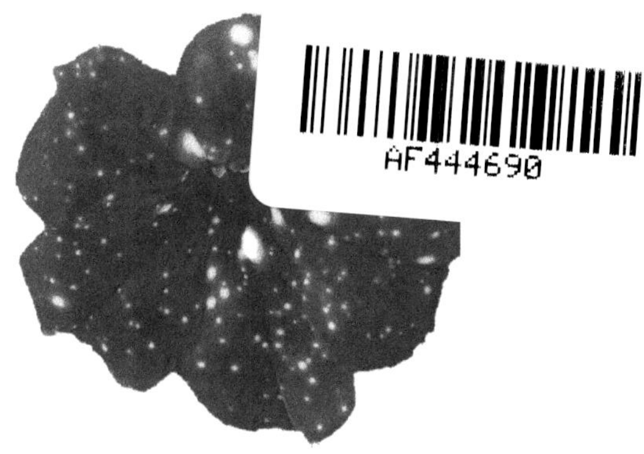

Poetry and Prose

By L. L. Tenderholt

My Vicissitudes

A Journey Through

Mental Illness * Becoming Estranged * Contentment

TENDERHOLT Creative

ISBN 979-8-9860320-0-9 (eBook edition)

ISBN 979-8-9860320-1-6 (paperback edition)

Published by Tenderholt Creative
Fargo, North Dakota
TenderholtCreative.com

To the one who still holds my hand,

and will never let it go.

Help Is Available

National Suicide Prevention Hotline

800-273-8255

CONTENTS

I found myself in a very strange place.

A place that was somewhere between a deep depression and recovery.

A place where I had lost so much but was learning to appreciate what I have.

A place of simultaneous healing and personal growth.

It was awful, freeing, painful, gross, awesome, lonely, difficult, wonderful, and maybe even worthwhile all at the same time.

Here is my experience.

Mood

There's No One Here

Be there for me
There's no one here
Hold my hand in the darkness
There's no one here
I don't know what matters
There's no one here
Keep my secrets hidden
There's no one here
Something just isn't right
There's no one here
I'm struggling along
There's no one here
I want to end it all
There's no one here
Ambivalent of my demise
There's no one here
My mind is sickness
There's no one here
I'm alone

L. L. Tenderholt

I'm Really Tired Today

I don't want
to come out and play
        I'm really tired today
I can't take a walk
It's just too much
        I'm really tired today
My soul aches
It's so very tired
        I'm really tired today

Depressed

I'm vaguely and acutely aware of time
It slips through my fingers while I stare at the numbers
I have to track all the things
Otherwise, it all gets lost in abyss

I feel like sunshine and roses for a day
The cleaning and washing and relationships get done
But then that cloud starts to darken
That doubting voice amplifies

I'm so tired and amped needing more energy
My momentum falters while I try to achieve balance
I stock my fridge with healthy things
Or else, I eat sugar like a junky

I practice gratitude breathing so deep
But the loss and the pain and the fear overwhelms
When will that ray of sunshine return?
I want to be normal for a day

L. L. Tenderholt

Tears

I tell you that I'm crying
That the stream of tears is hot
I fumble of the words
The grief wells up
The shame burns
I embrace the feelings
I wish you would hold me
It's hard to ask for what I want
Instead, I roll over
And close my eyes to sleep

Joy Drinks

They want to go drinking again
Bingo and beverages in a dark bar
I pull myself out of bed to shower
My arms get tired washing my hair
Strands of curls fall out in my hands

I can't drive so she picks me up
She always wants to get there early
Hoping to grab the coveted corner
He gets angry when she's there first
We order our heady joy in a glass

My mind struggles to make sense
Letters and numbers blur together
Wishing I could blame the joy drinks
I haven't touched my cup of cheer
The scramble of my mind fails me

I give in and sip the sweet sunshine
Dabbing away with bright pink circles
Dim light and worn wood are a comfort
Never quite belonging but blending in
Longing to go home and sleep again

L. L. Tenderholt

Self-Sabotage

I'm not worthy of anything
There's no reason to try
Failure
My family is better off
Let me list the reasons why
Loser
Hurting from the inside out
Prayers for relief surround me
Unfit
I truly can't do anything right
So please just let me be
Deadbeat
Sitting in the sun I'm cold
Isn't there anything more
Freak
I'll stay at home and ruminate
Wondering what it's all for
Defeat

I Can't

I can't even breath

There is no air

The ground fell away

I'm lying in a puddle

Bundle of nothing

No tears escape

Isn't it great?

Freedom to be me

Don't tell me what I need

I'll be alright

I'll be just fine

Just not tonight

L. L. Tenderholt

I Am So Damn Tired

A quick glance in the mirror

I can't look at myself long

My curls are a barometer

I haven't washed them lately

They are a fuzzy wild pile

I should brush my teeth

Before they rot and fall out

Maybe just clean clothes

But I haven't done laundry

I wonder if the girls ate

Better make sure they have

They'll be ok with noodles

I'll give them all that I have

Nothing left to help myself

Spinning

My mind
      Is whirling
            And spinning
                  I'm lost

I've learned
      To avoid
            Overeat
                  Drink a toast

How do
      I face this?
            Learning
                  To grow

My feelings
      Are haunted
            I'm crying
                  So low

L. L. Tenderholt

Advice

You should get up
I have soul crushing depression and anxiety
I need comfort and sleep and quiet

You should eat healthier
I have soul crushing depression and anxiety
I eat what I have energy to grab

You should exercise
I have soul crushing depression and anxiety
I miss being active, I just can't

You should clean something
I have soul crushing depression and anxiety
I want a clean house and I'm ashamed

You should come out for lunch
I have soul crushing depression and anxiety
Going out into public is a nightmare

You should get help
I have soul crushing depression and anxiety
I see a psychologist, a psychiatrist, have ECT
treatments, have gone through many med
changes, take my meds, reach out to my family,
use my lightbox, read self-help books, drink
water, practice gratitude, meditate, journal,
practice psychodynamic- cognitive behavioral-
dialectical behavior- interpersonal- therapy, and
enter the hospital when needed.

You should be grateful
I have soul crushing depression and anxiety
I just hope I'm tough enough to last another day

L. L. Tenderholt

Questioning

I'm wondering if I'll ever get better
If my days will be golden and filled with smiles
Will I ever find a baseline of happiness?
Will I make it through these miles?

Why can't I be happy?
Why can't I love like I once did?
Why has everyone left me?
Why can't I have a winning bid?

Can I find my way back to health?
To a body and mind that I love and admire?
Will I ever find a workable plan?
Will I hold myself to that fire?

I'm Alone

Yesterday, or a year ago, when time flies
I basked in your smiles and replies
Alone is the mood I cannot shake
Loneliness is the feeling at stake

Clouds overhead makes it dark inside
Forever is no promise when you lie
Our heart threads were strong enough
Strung together when times were tough

Tell me forgiveness is on the horizon
Suffocating in this bed that I lie in
Great tears fell when I missed our affair
From an original to not wanted there

L. L. Tenderholt

Pain

There's pain
All around
In my heart
In my back
In my mind

But there's hope
For better days
Rebuilding
Uplifting
Healing

Empty

Depression took me in its arms
        and brought deep into the darkness
I laid there knowing it was wrong
        and helpless to break free
There was no laughter
        and love was spread sparingly
I coveted it all to keep my face above water,
        but family is needy and deserving

Finally, they offered relief in drastic methods
        of voltage coursing through
Again, I laid there knowing it was wrong
        and helpless to break free
The toll is significant,
        but I continued warily
I let things go to keep myself afloat
        and family were hurt and leaving

And now our home is empty

L. L. Tenderholt

The Blue

(an ECT experience)

They stop me every time
Minding my business like its theirs
Holding me in a spotlight of nerves
Like a brilliant yellow light
But soon the blue will come
First, I have to play the game
I take my warm blanket
And the warm words
Holding them close as I wait and wait
But soon the blue will come
There is no warning
The warming pain hits my veins
Deep breaths ease the process
Inhale exhale, inhale exhale
But soon the blue will come
I wake disoriented
I stare at the faces peering back at me
I don't know who you are
I don't remember our home
Oh yes that blue has come

words

words are tricky things

They don't cooperate like they should

They don't mean what is said

I'm confused

I'm jumbled

I'm muddled

I'm disorganized

Fit in the box I want you to be in

Tell the story that my heart is bleeding

Sieve out the feelings inside

Make everything whole again

Everything Is Wrong

How is it even possible
To live through so much heartache
Broken into pieces
Time and time and time again

Pain doesn't make you stronger
It makes you darker
Wearing out your soul
Thin like an over washed fabric

Nothing left to give
No energy to take what I need
Lonely and all alone
The glitter is just grit in my eyes

Sadness

I feel it well
I can't cry
Tamp it down
So deep inside

It's not depression
It's just being sad
I can't handle it
Feelings are bad

What can I do
I have to evade
Avoid vibrations
Just let it fade

Hide under covers
Close my eyes
Take a deep breath
Release the sigh

Poke around inside
Is it gone?
The feeling may come
But it can't stay long

Atonement

My depression takes the best of me
It's often dark and deep
Affecting everyone and everything
As I withdraw and sleep

My emotions are often uncontrollable
I didn't know what to do
I get so overwhelmed sometimes
I didn't have a clue

My reaction has often been the worst
I thought that I knew best
That I was right at any cost
I was so obsessed

My apologies are not enough
I've really caused some pain
I can't take back what's happened
And "I'm sorry" is said in vain

My hope is that one day you'll see
I loved you in my way
That we can try to build again
And I can truly hear what you say

My atonement may never be complete
But I work on it every day
Trying to find what's wrong with me
And learn a better way

Oblivion

Can I go back to oblivion?
I'm tired of growing and being strong
Let me be clueless and traipse along
Childlike and marching to my own song

Can I go back to being carefree?
Where the only one I cared about was me
It seemed like the place to be
I was totally footloose and fancy free

L. L. Tenderholt

Enough

I want to be enough

Good enough

Strong enough

I want you to be proud

I want to be seen

I want to be invited

Asked along

Just called

I want to be wanted

I wish that you still cared

Please understand

Please empathize

I want to be heard

I want to be desired

Enough

Estranged

It Was Never Easy

It was never easy
Raising kids
I started too early
Just a kid myself
Hard cloudy days
I thought I was okay
Living life in a haze
Of mental illness
Always one step behind
Others were better
Nothing was fine
I tried so hard
Now things are silent
They are all gone
Stars out of alignment
I still love them

L. L. Tenderholt

Colors

I wish I could remember events how they actually went

Instead, the memories come in waves of colored emotions

Only snippets of the words in the peripheral of my mind

My depression was heavy and there were waves of black

Dark blue and purple threaded through dark feelings

You were frustrated that we hadn't talked in two weeks

And I said the wrong thing when I found energy to speak

There should have been words to soothe your suffering

Darkness bled through my muddy mind and broken heart

So instead of saying I love you and you mean everything

Hurtful words about nothing left to say came out instead

And part of me meant it because I was in so much pain

I wanted to fade into oblivion and leave you in the light

where you had a chance at living a life that eludes me

where struggles are bearable with a mind that is healthy

without sickness tainting your soft sweet stunning heart

I pray that your colors are brilliant shades of the rainbow

L. L. Tenderholt

Mother Isn't Here

She was gone
In a terrible way
Physically present
But lost in the darkness
Her children were clothed
There was always food
But that mothering spirit
Showed up sporadically
She was numb
Deep under covers
Or zoned out again
Hiding at the bar
Unable to hear
Self-absorbed
The kids needed more
They needed their mother

Mother's Day

It's Mother's Day
I spit the words out like venom
Concentrate
My mother needs flowers
Beautiful like her
Anxiety
Where will my children be?
From three to none
I hate today
Failure
I've done it all wrong
I loved being a mother
My heart is broken
I'm doing it wrong
How
I want to be the kitchen people love
To be peace and offer harmony
Enough
Glimmers of hope
But first I rage

Dream

I no longer hope
That you will come home
Those dreams have died

I need to move on
With what I have left
These dreams will grow

I no longer pray
That door has been closed
Those dreams have lied

I need to belong
With souls that inspire
These dreams will flow

I no longer trust
That family will be there
Those dreams have cried

I need to believe
With love in my heart
These dreams will glow

It

When your children divorce you, it leaves a void
And nothing you can do will fill it

You have to accept things and hold that reality
Work through the pain and face it

When you know that you're wrong, so very wrong
You've written the words and sent it

But they will not accept or open your text
Or return your call, you've done it

You've botched as a parent, your biggest fear
You've failed and you just can't deny it

Maybe someday when you are old and gray
They can find it inside to absolve it

L. L. Tenderholt

Gone

I'm finding some sunshine
My days aren't as long
Laughter sneaks past my lips
But the girls are gone

I'm taking better care
The laundry is getting done
I take pride in a shiny sink
But the girls are gone

I'm saying I love you
My friends are coming around
Plans are being made
But the girls are gone

I'm enjoying my garden
Books are getting read
Music is playing
But the girls are gone

Separation

I thought my heart would break

It should have

But it didn't

I didn't feel the rage

I panicked

I cried

But it's done

I never thought you'd leave

Something happened

You couldn't

Yet my heart it did not break

You are gone

But loved

Low

I feel low

Low and slow

I miss them

To the core

This is hell

An empty chasm

It's too deep

Too much pain

Days float by

I am alone

The quiet grows

I reach out

To thin air

Sick and sad

I don't care

Eyes

Black dress with beat up kicks
An awkward walk that draws attention
Proud moments
Don't shake hands
You spot me across the gym
I lower my eyes in shame
My cheeks are burning
Palms sweating
I try to think of something
Your eyes are blue

Rain

Rain pouring down
Damp heat all around
I start the laundry
I need to hear the sound

I taught them to hate
To disregard people
They don't talk to us now
They used to be gentle

The sky is so gray
It's gloomy outside
The laundry needs changing
It steadies my mind

Please

Won't you come to Easter
With family and food
Won't you come to Easter
Pretend you're in the mood

Won't you join our table
And tell us how you've been
Won't you join our table
You will still fit right in

Won't you please forgive me
I really said it wrong
Won't you please forgive me
It's really been too long

Won't you come to Easter
We can start again
Won't you come to Easter
And love us once again

L. L. Tenderholt

Reason

Give me a reason
To keep breathing this air
Our house is no home
With no one here

The rain doesn't stop
Not even a little
I put away the laundry
And try to settle

How can I fix this?
Runs through my mind
But it's really over
I know deep inside

Desolate

I wanted attention yes

I craved it like sunshine

Like air and water

My selfish ways

Interfering with my good intentions

Ego stripped us bare

And let out all the dreadful

While we plead for loveliness

Softness and blessings

Instead

We became desolate

Turn Around

I finally get to see you
My heart finds a happiness
My nerves do their flips
I count down the days
The time arrives

I enter the room
You're sitting on the sofa
I'm met with a stony glance
That quickly turns away
Today is not the day

There's no reconciliation
No desire for understanding
Apologies require space
But your walls are solid
And still

I'm so glad you are here
I let the words tumble out
It was so good to see you
You face the opposite wall
And grumble a fast reply

You run down the stairs
Escaping the awkwardness
I hope that next time
You will want to talk
But my heart would be happy

If you would just turn around

Lost Our Light

I look in every corner
And around every bend
There are only shadows
No light to show the way

Our daughters have left
They visit us no more
There is an emptiness
I don't know what to say

I cannot change the past
I can only change myself
Becoming a better person
It's a little price to pay

We pray they come around
They are welcome anytime
We think about them always
We wait until that day

L. L. Tenderholt

Quietly

I find the remote and turn off the T.V.

I just can't listen anymore

The air conditioner whirring is too loud anyway

The dog is lying with his eyes open

He doesn't blink

I ask him to blink if he's alive and he obliges

The neighbors are unusually silent

There's no laundry to do

The phone isn't ringing or pinging from messages

None of the children ever come home

Punishing with silence

Quietly I ponder if our family will ever be whole again

old

I'm not pretty anymore
Like a whisp of wind
Laughing at the day

I'm not young anymore
Heavy hips sway
Heart aches and pain

I'm not soft anymore
Settled like candy
Shards like glass

I'm not here anymore
Off on my own
Only and lonely

I'm not mom anymore
You're both gone
Yearning for you

Tea

My sister said to sit outside

I needed to leave my sighs in the wind

It was cold and I needed my cozy sweater

But the sun still shone through the leaves

During my travels I like to buy tea

I saved it so we could drink it together

The chair next to me is empty

I open the packet anyway

The only sweetness is honey

Open Spaces

People live in these wide-open spaces
But I live alone in this tiny cement room
There's no window to bring in the sunlight
It's dark and it's cold and it's full of gloom

I try to brighten it up with some color
But my lovely bright colors fade to grey
I try to leave and have some adventures
But I'm tired too early and I end my day

Back into bed I start thinking of them
I dream I say goodbye and run away
Part of me prays they catch up to me
Embracing they say they love me anyway

The reality is that they are better off gone
Living their lives in those big open spaces
My cement room is no place to grow up
But I lose many tears recalling their faces

I Love Letting Go

I'm learning some things
> *About myself*
> *About my family*

Lessons keep flowing
> *I keep growing*

I'm starting to heal
> *Getting strong*
> *Getting along*

Things are improving
> *Life keeps moving*

I've sent out my remorse
> *To my family*
> *To my friends*

One thing I know
> *I love letting go*

Pg 49

Im Sorry

Contentment

Simple

Tea on the balcony
One chore at a time
What's for supper
Waiting in line

These are the simple things
The things that keep me sane
These are the simple things
Soothing to my brain

Sitting in the rocking chair
Stretching for a moment
Walking the dogs
Working on atonement

These are the simple things
That get me through the day
These are the simple things
Keeping the blues away

L. L. Tenderholt

Limeade Afternoon

Sun dappled tree

Laundry in the dryer

Hair is still dripping

From the steamy hot shower

Birds are chirping

The dogs' tails are wagging

Smell of the candle

Music so soothing

Peaceful and quiet

A limeade afternoon

Dinner

What can I cook today?
The options are endless
Where is the cayenne
Minced garlic and butter

Chicken or fish
I love peas in my hotdish
Rice for days
It has to taste like something

A dash of love
Is there room for dessert?
Amazing and sweet
With a Bourbon glaze

3,247 Steps

I've been waking up tired
Feeling under, feeling low
Overwhelmed with to do's
Doubting myself, I'm slow

Simplicity has taken over
Unable to get it all done
Today is full of happy things
For me a marathon to run

The day starts to float away
And I have to scurry around
Trying to become presentable
My nerves are tightly wound

I push myself to go along
We go to lunch and shop
Slowly finding things we like
I'm thankful when we stop

Home I go to cook and clean
Thrilled they are on the way
There's too much left to finish
The rest we will have to delay

Dinner is all ready to go
When you arrive at our door
The chattering fills my heart
Time with you both I adore

And then the day is all done
We rest and then off to bed
3,247 steps seem like nothing
But I can't believe what I read

For me, it is an incredible win
A day that was full of doing
I drift off to sleep with a smile
My awful days are subduing

It's been a long hard road
Working through this ordeal
I'll take one step at a time
And maybe someday I'll heal

Plant

The best gift I've gotten
Is a little white planter
It has nine little pots
All in a cluster

I've bought up the herbs
And dug right in
It smells like a kitchen
When mama is cooking

I water the soil
It sets in the sun
Planting my herbs
Was my kind of fun

My Furry Friends

Laying in the sun without a care in the world

I envy your peaceful sleep

Sidling up as close as can be

Giving your love so freely

Interrupting my moments with soft soulful eyes

Loving me for who I am

Accepting the love I have to give

Simple moments of connection

Charlie

Black and gray
Salt and Pepper
Spice of my life
Sleeping at my feet
Sleeping by my chair
Sleeping the day away
Old brown eyes
Cloudy but sharp
Seeing it all
Old dog
Playing like a puppy
Until the moment passes

Sophie

Thick little white curls
Big beautiful brown eyes
Sass to the tips of her toes

Ask her "Where's dad?"
She's instantly alert
Obsessed with his attention

In charge of mealtime
There's no sneaking by her
And mind your manners too

Her favorite toys
Strewn across the floor
Until naptime overcomes

Gratitude

My heart was so heavy when I thought all was lost
Distorted thoughts were making my light feel dim
Tears would run down face while I choked out words
But what is the real truth he'd ask again and again

Reality is the hardest pill; I have to swallow it down
You have to accept all the gross and grime inside
The dirty little things that we want to keep quiet
I'll let go of my shame and move on with clear eyes

There may never be a chance to truly redeem myself
But my life is much more than multitudes of mistakes
I still have dreams of what the future could bring
I have memories to hold and a heart full of grace

So, I'll take a moment to give my dogs some love
I'll find inspiration in art, music, books and my life
When overwhelmed, I'll light a candle and breathe
Gratitude will warm me in good times and in strife

I Belong

Somewhere
I don't know where
There's a place
I feel safe in my skin
I know what to say
I'm welcome there
People love me
And people let me love them
As best I can
I'm looking to find it
I'll go there with you
Things will be ok
Somewhere
I belong

L. L. Tenderholt

The Robins Are Back

The robins are back
But it's still cold
It might just snow
The robins are back
The trees are still barren
The clouds are glum
The robins are back
They flit through the branches
But it's not really spring
The robins are back
They call to each other
I wish warm weather would come

Baking

The kitchen is warm

We dance around each other

Soft melodies play in the background

Familiar music of our youth

We're baking together

It smells a bit like heaven

The dogs are lying close

Happy to rest while we work

We talk about nothing

Words ebbing and flowing

We reminisce about older times

Remember the smells of our mother's kitchens

Sweet moments are savored

You steal a kiss

I feel some contentment

Enjoying the sweeter side of life

L. L. Tenderholt

Responsibility

I will take responsibility for me
My words, my actions and what I need
But I am the person I need to be
I need to be happy with what I see

I will take responsibility for my day
My thoughts, my excuses and what I say
But I am comfortable with who I am today
I need to continue to find my own way

I will not take responsibility for you
Your beliefs, your opinions and what you do
But I send you peace your whole day through
I need to focus on what's really true

Family Dinner

Uncle finds the chair closest to me and sits down

He puts his arm around my shoulders and says good to see you

Soon the menfolk find their way to our end of the table

I have no idea what they are talking about

I'm happy to just listen to the chatter and I nod and agree

The waitress brings my lemonade and fish and chips

My husband ordered fish and chips and a beer

One of the little ones tells me all about her barbeque sauce

While another one hangs off my husband's arm

The toddler is off with his parents in the game room

While his grandparents visit at the end of the table

The middle is filled in with cousins and nieces and nephews

Cozy comfortable conversations buzz up and down

Their beautiful faces are filled with smiles laughter and love

L. L. Tenderholt

Goodness

Somedays I need a reminder
Things aren't always so black and white
And your opinion is not the measure that I live by

I make so many mistakes
Sometimes I find myself saying things so wrong
And my mental illness exacerbates my reactions

Other times I do so well
The stars align and things are beautiful
Time spent together where we can enjoy each other

Feelings are such fickle things
So are the selections from our memories
What moonish mood do I want to wear today?

I am choosing contentment
While I work on myself and my pain
I wish you nothing but peace and happiness as well

I'm moving forward with my life
I'll accept the repercussion of my behavior
But I'll remember that there was goodness too

Maturity

It's hard to grow up
When you're 45
Stretching old brittle wings
Oh, look at the view

Quieting the pain
Blooming with self-love
There are colors in our soul
Beauty on the inside

Finishing what was started
No need to crow
Tasks are gratifying
Let's realize our dreams

Reality

Not every day is wonderful

    In fact, some of them are awful

    There are days that I still need to rest

    Those days are just not my best

    Some days I feel rather dark

    And my memories are quite stark

But others I'm moving along

    Like lyrics to my favorite song

    I find contentment in little things

    And embrace the bliss that it brings

    I work on the things that I can

    So that I can begin again

By my side

I wanted to leave

To run away

I planned my escape

I dreamed of the day

You never gave up

Standing aside

You held to hope

United and allied

Together we're learning

Day by day

New ways to love

And I want to stay

A future together

Letting go of pride

Thank you for staying

By my side

Reception

I can't find a thing to wear
Where did these last 20 lbs come from?
I dig out an old flowy skirt
And hide under an oversized tank top

I paint my nails in a brilliant purple
Adding little flower stickers here and there
I dig out my rose gold jewelry box
Because that's where I keep the good stuff

After a glance in the mirror, we head out
It's a half hour drive to the restaurant
Your daughter is just moments behind
Incredibly 17 and unwilling to ride with us

We find our seats with your family
You find your way up to the bar
But soon the waitresses take over
Making sure our beverages are fresh

The bride is breathtakingly beautiful
The groom looks so much in love
The children look happy with the marriage
A blended family based on faith and optimism

Your daughter agrees to a dance
She frolics around in her 4-inch heels
You've put aside your differences
And you smile at each other from the heart

Soon the family starts fade away
We hit the floor for a couple's dance
I love it when you hold me close
We chatter about the evening

Then we give our respects
We tell Aunt and Uncle it was wonderful
They tell us to visit them soon
It was really a pleasant evening

The drive home goes quickly
The summer air still holding its heat
We open the windows when we get home
So, the sweet breeze can carry us off to sleep

L. L. Tenderholt

Love

You listen to me natter on
And on and on and on
Words spew from deep inside
I want the world to be love and peace

We talk to dogs to fill the space
The void of our empty nest
Teasing and cajoling
Preparing for harder conversations

Your neck is my favorite place
I nestle in like it's sunshine
Soft kisses remind of back when
A reprieve from the struggles we face

Meals are taken together
Forget the table we sit on the sofas
Commenting on how good it is
My compliments to the chef

Let's take a walk and enjoy the air
Get out in the world and hold hands
And talk of all the things
We find normalcy together

Unfurl

I feel like I've come through the darkness

I'm finding myself in a place I've never been

I had been a mother my entire adult life

Now I have to find a new label for myself

My body aches but not as much as my soul

I crave the sweet sunshine and balmy breeze

It clears out the cobwebs left from that other life

I face the future with hope and contentment

What color wings have I earned in that darkness?

Will they be brilliant and pleasing to the eye?

Maybe they will be muted in browns and golds

A reflection of the regrets from that time

There are no warning signs to predict these things

No gypsy fortune teller to warn us of changes

We have to go through them when they come our way

Now I must pull my wings out of this cocoon and

unfurl

About the Author

L. L. Tenderholt's longest love affair has been with words. From a young age she loved to piece them together to express feelings and contemplate events. Her life has been a tapestry woven together by the rainbows of life's vicissitudes.

Many of her years have been spent fighting her demons, but there are also times of rest and even joy. L. L. Tenderholt enjoys spending time with her family, walking her dogs, watercolor painting, reading, and experiencing the world through travel.

website: tenderholtcreative.com/lltenderholt

Facebook: www.facebook.com/L.L.TenderholtAuthor

www.ingramcontent.com/pod-product-compliance
Lightning Source LLC
Chambersburg PA
CBHW061346140726
47997CB00003B/1084